50 THINGS TO KNOW ABOUT RUNNING A BUSINESS

PLAN, EXECUTE, AND SUCCEED

I0480465

Jennifer McGuire

CZYK Publishing Since 2011.

50 Things to Know

Lock Haven, PA
All rights reserved.
ISBN: 9798677168994

50 THINGS TO KNOW
BOOK SERIES
REVIEWS FROM READERS

I recently downloaded a couple of books from this series to read over the weekend thinking I would read just one or two. However, I so loved the books that I read all the six books I had downloaded in one go and ended up downloading a few more today. Written by different authors, the books offer practical advice on how you can perform or achieve certain goals in life, which in this case is how to have a better life.

The information is simple to digest and learn from, and is incredibly useful. There are also resources listed at the end of the book that you can use to get more information.

50 Things To Know To Have A Better Life: Self-Improvement Made Easy!

Author Dannii Cohen

This book is very helpful and provides simple tips on how to improve your everyday life. I found it to be useful in improving my overall attitude.

50 Things to Know For Your Mindfulness & Meditation Journey
Author Nina Edmondso

Quick read with 50 short and easy tips for what to think about before starting to homeschool.

50 Things to Know About Getting Started with Homeschool by Author Amanda Walton

I really enjoyed the voice of the narrator, she speaks in a soothing tone. The book is a really great reminder of things we might have known we could do during stressful times, but forgot over the years.

Author HarmonyHawaii

---

50 Things to Know to Manage Your Stress: Relieve The Pressure and Return The Joy To Your Life

Author Diane Whitbeck

There is so much waste in our society today. Everyone should be forced to read this book. I know I am passing it on to my family.

50 Things to Know to Downsize Your Life: How To Downsize, Organize, And Get Back to Basics

Author Lisa Rusczyk Ed. D.

Great book to get you motivated and understand why you may be losing motivation. Great for that person who wants to start getting healthy, or just for you when you need motivation while having an established workout routine.

50 Things To Know To Stick With A Workout: Motivational Tips To Start The New You Today

Author Sarah Hughes

50 THINGS TO KNOW ABOUT RUNNING A BUSINESS

BOOK DESCRIPTION

Have you been dreaming of owning your own company? Do you have a passion or hobby you would like to turn into profit? Are you tired of working for someone else?   If you answered yes to any of these questions, then this book is for you. 50 Things to Know about Running a Business by Jennifer McGuire, offers an approach to the steps it takes to run a successful company. Most books on running a business tell you that it's worth the reward. Although there's nothing wrong with that, they never go into the struggles you'll face financially, mentally, and possibly physically. Based on knowledge from leading experts, you'll learn how to face these struggles head on.

In these pages you'll discover tips to help you start and maintain a successful business. This book will help you determine if being a business owner is right for you.

By the time you finish this book, you will know the details and hard work entailed in running a company. So grab YOUR copy today. You'll be glad you did.

TABLE OF CONTENTS

50 Things to Know

Book Series

Reviews from Readers

BOOK DESCRIPTION

TABLE OF CONTENTS

About the Author

INTRODUCTION

1. Passion into Profit

2. Being the Boss

3. Signs It's Time to Be Your Own Boss

4. Read, Read, Read

5. Prepare a "Break-even" Analysis

6. Choosing a Business Name

7. Your Mission Statement

8. Don't Quit Your Day Job (Yet)

9. Know Your Numbers

10. Value Proposition

11. Start-up Financing

12. Permits and Licenses

13. Insurance

14. Marketing

15. Social Media

16. Company Website

17. Search Engine Optimization (SEOs)

18. Finding a Successful Location for Your Business

19. Hiring Employees

20. Firing Employees

21. Independent Contractors

22. Taxes

23. Bookkeeping

24. Accrual vs Cash Accounting

25. Pricing Strategy

26. Trade Shows

27. Networking

28. Supply and Demand

29. Partnerships

30. Types of Partnerships

31. Business to Business (B2B) Sales

32. Creating Value

33. Loytalty Programs

34. Investments

35. Time Management

36. Have a Routine

37. Working Long Hours

38. Build a Support Network

39. Invest in Yourself

40. Get Enough Sleep

41. Manage Your Emotions

42. Building Your Confidence

43. Having Motivation

44. Learn from Failures

45. Dealing with Cynics

46. Wearing Multiple Hats

47. Dealing with Lazy Employees

48. Customer Service Excellence

49. Cons of Running a Business

50. Pros of Being an Entrepreneur

50 Things to Know

ABOUT THE AUTHOR

Jennifer McGuire, a successful business owner for over 10 years, is currently living in Louisiana and doing work as a freelance editor and writer. When she is not writing and editing, she is working on building her second small business. With over 10 years of small business experience, Jennifer is well versed in entrepreneurism and enjoys helping others pursue their business dreams.

INTRODUCTION

"When I dare to be powerful - to use my strength in the service of my vision, then it becomes less and less important whether I'm afraid."

- Audre Lorde

Many people dream of running their own business, but few actually take the leap into the unknown. You're probably comfortable where you're at and afraid of failure, but overcoming those fears and boundaries is liberating. As an entrepreneur, you'll have the freedoms in life you don't have working a conventional job.

Being your own boss is one of the most rewarding careers and offers benefits many other careers don't provide. As a successful business owner, you'll have a stable salary and flexible time with your family. Yes, you'll be taking a risk, but wouldn't you rather take a chance on yourself rather than spend your life making someone else's dream come true?

If you feel like there's more to life and you want to do something meaningful, then it's time for you to give it a try! Remember, although there are highlights to running a business, there are also lowlights. Although starting a company is challenging, it's not impossible!

1. PASSION INTO PROFIT

Running a business should be exciting and profitable. Choose something you enjoy doing! There will be challenges to make a success of a small company if it doesn't interest you. You wouldn't want to own a lawn care business when your heart is really in dog grooming. Determine something you're really enthusiastic about and turn it into a lively business venture.

You will need to choose a product or service you know confidently and intimately. Trying to master a new skill or industry while trying to get your business running will only add unnecessary pressure and lower your chances of success. Sure, it may be fun to run a bakery, but if you've spent the last 5 years making homemade candles and don't have any experience with baking cakes, you are probably better off starting a candle making business.

There are so many kinds of people and an array of different businesses. Giving distinct advice on the precise type of business you should start is difficult. Only you will be able to answer that question.

2. BEING THE BOSS

Entrepreneurism is a rollercoaster adventure full of ups and downs. As challenging as it is, the rewards are bountiful. Running a company is exciting yet daunting, so it's imperative that you can handle stress well. Owning a business can be stressful but absolutely doable. Reaping the awards makes it well worth it.

Being your own boss doesn't mean you're excluded from having responsibilities. There will still be projections to be completed, deadlines to meet, and bookkeeping to keep updated and balanced. Something will always need to be taken care of.

The best advice is to stay on top of your obligations. Remember to focus on setting and keeping deadlines, fulfilling your projections, and following a schedule. You don't want to get so far behind that you start to lose control.

3. SIGNS IT'S TIME TO BE YOUR OWN BOSS

Being your own boss may sound attractive, but it's difficult to consider making that jump from comfortable paycheck into the unknown. Maybe you've been contemplating starting a business but you keep thinking, "It's not the right time", "I'm too young/old", "What if I fail?" Fear is normal and you can't let it keep you from dreaming big.

If the itch of being an entrepreneur has been nagging at you for years, it may be time to take the plunge. You might be full of anxious questions and lack confidence in yourself at first, but stop trying to convince yourself not to go for it. There will always be a reason not to do something, but if the thought of running a company isn't a fleeting one, then that's a sign to keep pushing forward.

Working for someone else, you've probably been climbing that corporate ladder. Maybe you are successful by society's measure, but your job isn't providing you with the gratification you desire. Or perhaps you've been in a rut and can't seem to get any further ahead. Getting up every day to head to work feels like a chore, and you live for weekends and vacations. You look around your office whispering to yourself "there must be more". These are the moments you realize you are ready to go off on your own and take charge of your life and career.

If every day feels like Groundhog Day and you feel like pulling your hair out, it could be a sign it's time to be your own boss. You feel suffocated, and the job is draining the energy and inspiration out of you. You want to be in the driver's seat and have more control over your future.

You may feel like a square peg trying to be shoved into a round hole. Getting further and further from the real you can take a toll. A great deal of energy is required to play a role at work. You feel like you have to be a different person at work to succeed. Work may also be leaving you frustrated and angry. This hostility could eventually affect your personal relationships.

If any of this sounds like you, you may be destined to be your own boss! If your dream is to run your own company, don't let it go! Stop putting it off due to fear. Turn that fear into excitement and let it propel you into a brighter future!

4. READ, READ, READ

Read as much as possible and absorb as much information as you can about the kind of business you're wanting to start. There are so many different kinds of books to help you on your journey through entrepreneurialism. You can get a better understanding on what you should expect by reading books from successful business owners.

Blogs are another good source of reading materials. There are countless business blogs revolving around the ins and outs of running a company. Simply do a web search for "business blogs" and you'll find a flood of different informational blogs to help expand your knowledge.

Learning is essential in any endeavor. The most successful people are the ones who have a passion for learning and growing. Try to make it a habit to read a different book every couple of months or so.

5. PREPARE A "BREAK-EVEN" ANALYSIS

Finding your niche in a sea of endless business ventures may be difficult, but it's not impossible. How do you know if your business idea will be profitable? Honestly, there is no way to be sure, but that shouldn't stop you from doing some research on the financial soundness of your ideas. First thing you should do is prepare a break-even analysis to get an idea of success of that business idea.

The analysis shows you the amount of revenue you'll need to cover your expenses before you make a profit. If you can reach and surpass your break-even point, then you have a good chance of having a profitable business.

You must make educated guesses about the expenses and revenues and do some serious research to determine your sales volume and expenses. You will need to do the following calculations and estimates:

Fixed Costs: Fixed costs, or sometimes called "overhead", don't fluctuate much from month to month. These costs include utilities, rent, insurance and other set expenses. It's always a smart idea to add

10% into the analysis to cover expenses you can't predict.

Sales Revenue: You need to base the forecast on the volume of business you really expect and not on how much you need to make a profit. This will be the total dollars from sales you bring into your business each year or month.

Average Gross Profit for Each Sale: The average gross profit is the money left from each sales dollar after paying direct costs of a sale. The direct costs are what is paid to provide your service or product. For example, if Mary pays an average of $200 for goods to make jewelry that she sells for an average of $400, her gross profit is $200.

Average Gross Profit Percentage: This percentage will tell you how much of each dollar of sales income is gross profit. In order to calculate that percentage, divide your average gross profit by the average selling price. For example, if Mary makes an average gross profit of $200 on jewelry she sells for an average of $400, her gross profit percentage is 50% ($200 divided by $400).

Once those calculations are complete, it's fairly easy to figure out your break-even point. Divide the estimated fixed costs by the gross profit percentage to determine the amount of sales and earnings you will need to bring in just to break even. For example, if Mary's fixed costs are $5,000 a month and her expected profit margin is 50%, her break-even point is $10,000 in sales revenue per month ($5,000 divided by 50%). Mary must make $10,000 each month just to pay her fixed costs and product costs. This number is not including profit or salary for Mary.

If you can't seem to break even, you will need to change certain aspects of your plan. Ways to do that are:

Work from your home to save rent/mortgage on a brick and mortar store.

Sell your service or product at higher prices

Don't hire employees

Find less expensive sources of supplies

Performing that break-even analysis can seem daunting at first. The good news is that the analysis is part of every business venture. If you start by doing a break-even analysis now, you'll have already started on your plan for success.

6. CHOOSING A BUSINESS NAME

After hours and hours of brainstorming for the perfect business name, you think you finally have it! However, never get too excited until you have conducted some research on trademarks and a name to make sure no one else is using it. Checking with your county clerk's office is also helpful when trying to find out if your proposed name is already on the list of assumed business or fictitious names in your county.

A "fictitious business name", or "assumed business name", is used when a company uses a name that's different from its "legal name". For example, if Mary Smith names her business Monarch Candles, that name would be considered a fictitious business because it does not contain Mary Smith's last name. You must register with your local county clerk's office if your business uses a fictitious business name. The "legal name" of a business is the official name of the individual that owns a business. If you are the only owner of the company, then its legal name is your full name.

Finding the best name for your enterprise depends on a plethora of considerations. Some ideas are as

obvious as the sort of company you have and others as particular as your own style and tastes. A favorable business name should:
- distinguish you from your competitors
- suggest the products or services you offer
- be original
- be catchy
- be clearly pronounced and spelled

7. YOUR MISSION STATEMENT

A well-crafted mission statement focuses the business for both employees and the target audience, and it serves as a framework as a launching point to build from when establishing the brand. The mission statement articulates the purpose of the business. That makes it a very important part of any brand building plan.

There are 4 key elements to focus on when writing your mission statement.
- Value - What is the value of the business to both customers and employees?
- Plausibility - Make it sound clear and reasonable
- Inspiration - Why should people want to work for the company?

- Specificity - Tie it back to the business

There are many opinions on how to create a perfect mission statement, but there are some clear do's and don'ts to consider. Keep it short and concise. Your mission statement should be summed up in just a few sentences. Think long term and keep it open enough to reflect your long-term goals. You don't want to limit your business. Leave some room for the business to grow into something different in the future, if needed. However, don't be afraid to change the statement if it no longer represents the company.

A mission statement is a declaration of what makes your business important. By design, it guides the actions of the employees and draws in customers by establishing order by explaining what the company intends to accomplish. For the consumers, it sets the company apart from the competition.

8. DON'T QUIT YOUR DAY JOB (YET)

The "all or nothing" strategy to starting a business is incredibly high risk and is usually the wrong path. Start working on your business plans while still maintaining your current job. A slow buildup ensures a preserved salary level and the financial commitments with the new venture.

When you're reliant on your new business to develop revenue, most likely you'll have to accept undesirable or low paying gigs. In the beginning stages of your entrepreneurial career, you may need to welcome short-term projects or work on building inventory if you sell products. If money isn't your primary concern at first, you can be more scrupulous in the jobs you obtain and avoid questionable clients and low margin work.

A side hustle adds excitement to what might feel like monotonous activities in your day job. The financial security allowed by your day job helps cultivate perspective. There will be setbacks, but it won't be life or death. Working in both territories enables you to tap into the creative joy of learning and experimenting while not getting lost in financial constraints.

9. KNOW YOUR NUMBERS

Before starting a business, you need to have a concrete financial plan. Start small and never assume your idea will be successful. Test your idea in a small, inexpensive way that gives you a good inkling of whether customers need your product or service and how much they're willing to pay for it.

Every type of business has its own financing needs, but it's been estimated that an entrepreneur will need six months' worth of costs on hand at start-up. Don't underestimate the costs of expenses. You should be more definite when planning your fixed expenses. One of the main reasons small companies fail is that they run out of money. Overestimating the company's revenue and underestimating costs is detrimental to a small business.

There is a small quantity of smaller activities that effect larger results such as average price per sale, proposal close rate, number of outbound sales calls, and number of live connections. Most business owners don't know what to fix to see an improvement when they see sales are low. By tracking each of those numbers, you can instantly know what to fix.

These numbers will also pinpoint what is working well.

Many entrepreneurs have a crummy sales month, then look back to determine what caused it. However, had he tracked his numbers on the underlying issues, he could have fixed the issue earlier. By tracking and understanding the numbers, you can measure whether your business is operating well.

10. VALUE PROPOSITION

A value proposition is a guarantee of value to be delivered and it's the primary reason a prospect should purchase from you. Your value proposition has to be the first thing visitors see on the homepage of your website and should also be visible at all major entry points to the site. The less known your business is, the better your value proposition needs to be.

A value proposition is a clear statement that offers relevancy, differentiation, and quantified value. Your value proposition should do the following: explain how your product solves a customers' problems or improves their situation, deliver specific benefits, and tell the customer why they should buy from you instead of the competition. The best value proposition is clear and easy to understand.

If all things are pretty much the same between you and your competitors, you can win by offering value-adds. Think what small things you could add that wouldn't cost you much but could be appealing to some buyers. You could offer free shipping, free bonus with purchase, discounted price, free setup, etc. Make sure these value-adds are visible with the rest of the value proposition.

11. START-UP FINANCING

There are many ways to find investments for your up-and-coming business. Are you wanting to invest your own savings into the business? Will you be asking family and friends for a minor investment? Or, would you like to get an experienced investor to become a shareholder? You can also work on getting a business loan from a local bank or even a government grant. Below are some ideas to get you started on finding funding.

- Personal Savings: Put your money where your mouth is and start by funding those early steps on your own, if possible. Funding your own start-up is always a good sign to investors. It shows that you are truly invested in the venture and they are more likely to help you if you prove you're willing to risk your own money.

- The Business: If at all possible, it's best to let the business pay for itself and let it grow from the revenue coming in. This is actually the best type of funding, but the dilemma here would be timing. Expenses commonly come before revenue, therefore you need to find a way to get cash up front. Working with prepaid orders is a great way to get this done. This will allow you to keep absolute control, and it's a continual reminder of the importance of sales. Although this is the preferable way to find funding, it can be a vigorous way to go. The growth of the business can be critically limited, while the pressure of fulfilling promised orders can be enormous.

- Government Grants: Grants are not widely advertised so finding the right one may be difficult but it doesn't make it impossible. Find official information on these grants and subscribe to their newsletters so you'll be aware when new applications open. Grants tend to be very region-specific, so make sure to correctly gauge the possibilities in your area. Grants require you to be extremely detailed on how the money will be spent and will have different degrees of control afterwards. The added layer of control may limit your room to veer later.

- Family and Friends: Starting off, there may not be very many people who believe in you. Hopefully, your friends and family will have enough faith in your dreams and will be willing to help you get your business off the ground. This makes it an attractive source of startup funding, however, if it's not done correctly it can blow up in more ways than one. It's fairly common for friends or family loans to result in resentment, fallouts, and lawsuits. Make sure you know the characters of the people involved and consider the possibilities if things go wrong. Be clear on the expectations. Are they giving you the money as a gift or do they want to share in the profits? Write the terms on paper and be concise on what they will be.

- Bank Loans: Bank loans are a common source for start-up funding, but in order to get a loan, you will need to convince the bank of the growth of your project and your capability to pay back the loan without any issues. The bank will focus on your cash flow, which is not always a fit for startups. You will have to repay the loan, including interest within the acknowledged time period. Failure to repay the loan might lead to bankruptcy. Make sure with any financing you receive, that you write up or sign a contract with very clear terms and always do your research first!

12. PERMITS AND LICENSES

When starting a business, the state will require you to get a ream of permits, tax registrations, licenses, among other requirements. Professional licenses are given to people practicing traditional professions such as doctors, lawyers, teachers, and accountants. States also license people in a vast range of trades, from real estate agents to auto mechanics.

Licensing procedures will alter, but you'll most likely have to show proof of training in the field and you may have to pass a written exam. In some cases, you may have to practice your profession under the guidance of a more experienced person before you can become completely licensed. Some licenses will be good for a period of time before retesting, while others require continuing education. If you make or sell products such as food, gas, liquor, and lottery tickets, the state may also want you to get a license.

There is such a collection of licenses and permits, it can be mind-boggling at times. However, you'll need to acquire them before opening the doors of your business. In order to be compliant of all laws and requirements, do diligent research of your state's provisions.

13. INSURANCE

Every business owner needs insurance to make sure they're protected against all the risks your business faces. Equipment, tools, materials, and technologies will all be things you need to keep your company running. Without the right small business insurance, you would have to front the costs of liability claims on your own. When you consider the average paid liability claim is around $15,000, you know that can be hard to cover.

A great policy to have is a Business Owner's Policy, and it combines business liability insurance and business property into one policy. This kind of policy offers several insurance products rolling into one. Business interruption, liability, and property insurance are typically included. However, most policies demand businesses to meet certain touchstones to qualify. Not all businesses meet the requirements for business owner's policies which may include revenue, class of business, size of the location, and business location.

Every business faces risks of liability claims, which is why getting the right business liability insurance is crucial. To help pay for lawsuits that claim your business caused property damage or bodily injury, you'll want general liability insurance. On the other hand, professional liability insurance helps cover lawsuits that claim you made omissions or errors in the services your business provides. You'll need to be covered by both of these insurance plans to protect your company.

14. MARKETING

Marketing is a major component of running a business. Having a clear perception of your customer base will boost your chances of having a successful enterprise. Business owners often make the blunder of defining their customer base too broadly, and that makes it challenging to engage in efficient marketing endeavors. You will need to determine a strong definition of your target customer because that will be the foundation for all of your marketing plans.

Many new entrepreneurs refuse to define a target customer base, believing it may narrow the business or weaken the number of potential customers, but this is a fallacy. Doing so does not prevent your business from accepting customers that don't fit the target profile. If a customer seeks your service or product, you will still be available.

Researching your competition is another aspect of marketing research. If you're selling a product or service, check out your competitor's prices and make yours comparable. Search their social networking sites, their websites, and other social networks to find what is working for them. This doesn't mean you need to copy their plan, but it gives you a good idea on where to start.

Strategies to consider when marketing:
- Website
- Print media, directories
- Sales letters, brochures, flyers
- Networking - go where your market is
- Direct/personal selling
- Press releases/publicity

Researching your markets and competition will determine your particular positioning, which will put you in a much better situation to promote and sell your product or service. Establishing goals for your marketing campaign can help you better understand whether or not your efforts are achieving results through ongoing review and evaluation of results. Fruitful marketers frequently review the status of their campaigns against their set objectives. This establishes ongoing improvements to your marketing initiatives and helps with future planning.

15. SOCIAL MEDIA

People are spending more and more time on their phones, and most of that time is spent on social media platforms. Social media users frequently interact with businesses they are interested in or already do business with. Not only is social media free, but your customers are already there waiting to hear from you.

For small companies concentrated on individual customers and community, this makes social media a dynamic platform for connecting with an audience to build brand loyalty and awareness. You can create the content and resources that will maintain added value to your customers and prospects. Try sharing a few different types of content and see what resonates well with your target audience. Once you've discovered the types of content your audience responds to, keep sharing in that way.

One of the most important aspects of executing your social media strategy will be tracking your progress. Based on your account performance, you will be able to make knowledgeable decisions about the direction of your campaigns. There are many different social media tools to help you manage your accounts, monitor engagement, and even advertise on the platforms.

16. COMPANY WEBSITE

Marketing is one of the most important aspects of your business, and a website is a great marketing tool. Building a website can be exciting and a bit intimidating. Start by familiarizing yourself with a few important aspects. This will make building your website easier and more efficient.

With a website, you want to have a clear intention as to what you are looking to achieve. Common website goals include increasing online sales, generating phone calls and leads, and booking appointments, consultations, and reservations, among other things.

You'll need to decide if you want to build it yourself or hire someone to do it for you. Building a website isn't as challenging as it used to be and it's possible for nearly anyone to build an attractive site these days. If you're on a tight budget, want full control of the site, and have the time to commit to the building process you could consider designing the website yourself. Hiring a professional almost guarantees the perfect website, but it usually comes at a high price tag. If you can afford the price and are too busy to put in the work yourself, hiring a designer would be a smart decision.

Despite the type of industry you're in, your website needs to tell visitors what your company offers. You must also include a way for visitors to get in touch, and the most common way to do this is with a contact form. Having a good understanding of who your audience is, how they're finding your site, and what they're looking to gain from visiting it, will help in beginning to understand how to design a site that best serves them.

17. SEARCH ENGINE OPTIMIZATION (SEOS)

If you have a website for your business, you probably already know the struggles of dealing with SEOs. Search engine optimization is the process of making your website rank for enticing keywords in order to bring in search traffic. What it boils down to is creating digital content that your audience wants to read and share.

You've probably come across the phrase "content is king" if you've spent any time reading about small business SEO and content strategy. However, not everyone can be king and not every piece of content can upgrade your search engine ranking. In fact, shoddy or vapid content can actually hurt your search engine results and drive away leads. Content only works when it relates to your audience, so it needs to be well written and well targeted.

New businesses don't usually show up on page one of Google's search engine for anything except some local searches or branded searches (a search for your brand name or name of a product you offer). You can climb up with good SEO and content marketing, but it has to be steady. You can't just heave out blog posts about everything you do and hope traffic pops up. You'll have to show Google you have authority in an area by targeting a precise range of topics and related keywords. You should set up a Google Analytic's account to track your success and records everything that happens on your site. After a few months, you'll get a baseline view of your audience base, which you can use to gauge your SEO performance.

18. FINDING A SUCCESSFUL LOCATION FOR YOUR BUSINESS

When trying to pick an effective location, determine the factors that will develop customer volume for your business. Will customers drive, and if so, where will they park or will they come on foot? Will more customers come if you are located near other small businesses? Will the reputation of the neighborhood help draw customers?

One important concern when searching for a commercial space is finding a place you can financially manage. Most start-up business owners don't have the funds to purchase real estate, so they opt for leasing a space.

Research average rental costs in your area to make sure the amount you allocated for rent makes sense. If you determined that the location is paramount to your business, be sure your budget will grant you the ability to rent suitable space given the average cost of space in your area.

The biggest consideration is occasionally not where it is but what it is when choosing a business space. The building needs to be fitting, or adaptable to, your business. For example, if you're planning to open a bakery, you need a space with kitchen facilities. Except for convincing the landlord to put in the necessary equipment, it's extremely unlikely that laying out the money yourself will be worth it. Zoning rules, parking, communications wiring, electricity, and air conditioning are all factors to consider when selecting the right place for your business.

Working from home can be simpler than leasing a separate office. However, it may put you in violation of laws that govern residential and business spaces.

Be sure you're knowledgeable of the laws that influence home businesses, as well as other issues such as home-office tax deduction.

19. HIRING EMPLOYEES

Before hiring just anyone, you need to understand what extra manpower entails. You'll have to deal with a whole new string of paperwork, liabilities, legal obligations, and expenses. It cost money to invest in hiring a new employee. Also, hiring mismatches can result in workplace violence, theft, and high turnover resulting in substantial costs to the company's reputation.

Understand that under-qualified, criminal, and emotionally unstable minds hid in all job titles. If your staff member's actions hurt someone, you can be held accountable. A background check will be necessary in the hiring process. The search usually consists of credit history, drug tests, driving record, criminal records, and confirmation of prior employment. Testing for illegal substances is also a good way to weed out weak links from your work environment. Pre-employment and random drug tests are an employer's best lines of defense.

Before making a formal offer, be sure to ask for at least three references. It's best for those to be professional references from past employers or mentors. You'd be surprised what you could learn from those phone calls. Once you've chosen the right person, there's a folder's worth of records you'll need to have completed before the newest team member can start work.

20. FIRING EMPLOYEES

Firing an employee is probably one of the hardest things you'll have to do as a business owner. The situation will be upsetting for both parties, no matter the reason for termination. Be clear on the reasons you are firing someone. Is the company downsizing? Did the employee perform poorly? Being as clear as possible is always best, but don't drag out the unpleasant task. Get to the point as quickly and concisely as possible.

Humiliating someone is never a good idea, so remember to treat them with dignity and give them the bad news privately and politely. You'll also want to avoid a scene. Troublesome reactions and uncomfortable scenes are bad for the rest of your employees and morale. Delivering the news at the end of the workday is a good way to avoid this situation.

Make sure there is a representative with you when you're firing an employee. This will help prove you legally and ethically terminated the employee in the case the employee files a legal suit against you. Firing an employee correctly is very important to your business. Having all the correct paperwork, including a termination letter, and knowing what to say is helpful when preparing to have that conversation. An employment letter will insure the terms are clear, including notice period and termination date.

21. INDEPENDENT CONTRACTORS

Many small business owners prefer to work with independent contractors rather than hiring employees. An independent contractor is someone who does work for another person or company. They are usually business owners who are in a trade, profession, or business and offer their services to the general public.

You may prefer to hire a contractor when you need something done quickly and need someone with specific skills and expertise. You'll probably pay more per hour or per job with a contractor, you could save money overall if you get someone who does the job skillfully. You don't need to commit to a salary and you're not required to pay them benefits.

Although there will be less paperwork involved with hiring a contractor instead of an employee, you will still have to have them sign some tax forms before work can be started. All contractors must sign a W-9 form, a new hire form, and a business contract. If you don't properly classify a worker, you may be fined, penalized, or end up in court, so it's always good to talk to a lawyer or accountant to get a second opinion.

22. TAXES

The thought of doing taxes is never a fun one, but it's a necessary evil that must be handled. Being a business owner can make your tax situation less straightforward than with traditional employment. The kind of entity you do business as, the type of product or service you sell, your role in the business, and where you do business are all factors that impact whom you pay taxes to and how you pay them. In most states, companies that sell products must set up a system where they charge the customers sales tax, collect that tax, and pay it to the state. Some services may also be subject to sales tax depending on the state law. Every state has its own tax laws, so it's fundamental that you understand what you state's reporting, collecting, and payment specifications are.

If you have employees, there are employment and payroll taxes. Employment taxes can be perplexing. You're required to collect, report, and pay payroll taxes on your employee's wages. These employment taxes get paid to the Social Security Administration, medicare taxes, state and federal unemployment taxes, and the IRS. Failure to file and pay may cause penalties, and sometimes criminal prosecution.

You may be responsible for self-employment taxes if you are self-employed. Self-employment taxes are for Medicare and Social Security. Since you wouldn't be receiving a paycheck withholding the Social Security and Medicare, self-employment tax is the alternative.

Keep very detailed records of how much money your enterprise earns and spends. This is a crucial step for you to plan and save for taxes. Hire a professional, arrange an accountant to review your work periodically, or do the bookkeeping yourself. You can start saving for income taxes once you begin tracking the income. Open a separate bank account precisely for your income taxes. The general rule of thumb is to save between 15-40% of your income for taxes.

"Estimated taxes" are income taxes that you pay every quarter. State and Federal quarterly estimated tax payments in April, June, September, and January of each year. You must pay income as you earn it, like an employee would with a paycheck. The amount you pay each quarter is an appraisal of what you think your taxable income at the end of the year will be. Accountants will often use last year's earnings as a base point.

23. BOOKKEEPING

If you have never considered yourself to be a "math person", the thought of learning bookkeeping isn't too exciting. As overwhelming as it seems, you need to be at least a little skilled in the art of bookkeeping if you want to run a successful business.

1. Assets, which are the resources and cash owned by the company. For example, inventory and accounts receivable.

2. Income or revenues, which is the money earned by the business, usually through sales.

3. Expenses, which is the cash that flows from the company to pay for items or services such as salaries and utilities.

4. Liabilities, which are debts and commitments owed by the business like loans and accounts payable.

5. Equity, which is the amount remaining after liabilities are deducted from assets, defining the

owner's interest in the business. For example, retained earnings and stock.

By now, most companies use computer software to do their bookkeeping. This virtual record is called the general ledger. Spreadsheet software such as Excel or Google sheets is usually the most economical choice. However, trying to create your own general ledger in a spreadsheet program could spin out of control very quickly.

Bookkeeping on desktop software commonly requires a costly up-front fee, but you get to keep the software. Online cloud-based bookkeeping comes at a cheaper cost than that of desktop software, but you have to pay a monthly fee to keep your subscription. Or, you can hire someone to manage your ledger and accounts for you.

Keep a record of every transaction and make sure it's recorded correctly and in the right account or your balances won't match. When you total up account credits and debits, the totals should match. This is when your books are "balanced".

24. ACCRUAL VS CASH ACCOUNTING

There are two principal methods of keeping track of a business's income and expenses. The cash method and the accrual method vary only in the timing of when transactions are debited or credited to your accounts. In most cases, you can decide which approach to take.

The cash method (also called cash basis) is the more generally used practice of accounting in small businesses. With this process, income is not counted until cash or a check is actually received and costs are not counted until they are paid. Though the cash method yields a more correct figure of how much actual cash your business has, it might bid a false picture of longer-term profitability. For instance, your records may show one month to be notably profitable when sales have been slow and a lot of credit customers paid their bill that month.

Under the accrual method, transactions are counted when the order is made, the services occur, or the item is delivered, regardless of when the money is actually received. Income is counted when the sale occurs and expenses are counted when you receive the goods or services. You don't have to wait until you see the money, or pay out of your checking account, to document a transaction.

25. PRICING STRATEGY

When establishing a business plan, entrepreneurs often make the blunder of setting their pricing strategy to match the lowest-price provider in the market. Early in the life of your small company, research your proposed market as thoroughly as possible. Pay close attention to past fluctuations in demand and competition.

Don't solely look at your competition's pricing. Look at the whole value of what they're offering. What are the value-added services? Are they playing to an affluent niche or price-conscious consumers? How do you compare? Having the lowest price is not a strong pricing strategy for small businesses. Customers would see your product or service as a commodity and that would cloud the value of your offering.

Research and analyze the different variables, such as ceiling price and price elasticity. The ceiling price is the highest price the market will carry. This can be examined by surveying consumers and experts and asking questions regarding price limits. However, the highest price available on the market may not be the ceiling price. Another variable to research is price elasticity. The price elasticity method shows the receptiveness of the demand of a service or product when nothing changes except the price. Some products have a more prompt and startling response to price changes. This usually happens when that product or service is considered non-essential, or because there are many substitutes.

Once you understand the demand in your market, review your own costs, supply chain, and profit goals as a way to inform your choice of strategy. Below are a handful of pricing designs to consider:

- Cost-Plus Pricing: The selling price is determined by adding a markup to the unit cost.

- Competitive Pricing:: Setting a price based on the price of the competition.

- Value Based Pricing: The price is based on the perceived or estimated value of a product or service.

- Price Skimming: Setting the price high initially and then lowering as competitors enter the market.

- Penetration Pricing: The price is set low to rapidly enter a competitive market and provoke word-of-mouth recommendations, only to be raised later.

Regardless of which strategy you choose, pricing your inventory correctly is essential for a successful business. You may have the most amazing product in the world, but if you can't price your products effectively, your sales will ultimately struggle.

26. TRADE SHOWS

Trade shows can be seen as an outdated business tool, but nothing could be further from the truth. Building relationships with partners, prospects, and customers is essential for business owners in today's competitive business environment. People want to do business with companies that have more of a "human touch" even if the vast bulk of their business is handled online.

Trade shows offer plenty of face time with other entrepreneurs in your industry and also with motivated, interested, potential clients. People attend these trade shows because they are responsive in what you have to offer and are more likely to listen to pitches, network with you, or even purchase your product or services. Trade shows continue to be one of the highest "return on investment" marketing channels for face-to-face interaction.

Trade shows require months of groundwork. Booths need to be designed and built weeks in advance. You need to refine your sales pitches and presentations and make sure you are well prepared. Unfamiliar small businesses and start-ups can use these events to declare themselves to the market and increase the credibility they have, so it's necessary to put your best foot forward.

27. NETWORKING

Interacting with potential clients, business partners, and investors will help you harvest trusting and loyal relationships and launch new opportunities. Making vital connections is vital for small business owners.

One way to network is to create a business page showcasing your company on LinkedIn. Connect your email, and you will automatically be able to add your contacts. You can search for contacts via their name or the company they work for, as well. LinkedIn is a networking platform allowing users to create groups by interest or industry, where you can connect to like-minded entrepreneurs and clients.

Cross-promotion is another significant way to make connections. Partner with another company, preferably not in your industry to dodge competition, and work together to promote each other's brands. You call leave coupons or flyer in each other's locations. By joining another business in your networking attempts, you can decrease your advertising and marketing cost and display your brand to a fresh customer base.

28. SUPPLY AND DEMAND

A business owner must always be thinking in terms of supply and demand. "Supply and demand" is focused on how much people want a particular product and how much of that product a company can drive to market. Supply and demand affect pricing and the volume of goods that are traded in the markets. The rarer the product, the more a business can charge for it.

The supply side refers to how much of a product can be supplied to buyers and at what price. There's no rationale for pricing an item artificially low if you don't have the manufacturing output to keep up with the spike in demand of people who want to get it at the low price. The order of demand states that all other factors being equal, demand will be reduced as the price of a product is raised. The business owner is responsible for finding the pricing sweet spot that will create as much of a profit as possible without causing demand to retract.

Using easily available supplies assures that a business will not pay too much for materials, permitting it to either keep prices low or increase profits. Using scarce materials that customers see as valuable by virtue of their scarcity allows a company to charge higher prices. In addition to these considerations, supply and demand affect decisions by influencing what businesses purchase, even making it more or less attainable for a business to use a particular raw material.

29. PARTNERSHIPS

Most times, people tend to rush into business together with little planning and ground rules. Taking on business partners should be reserved for when it's critical for the success of your company. First, you need to ask yourself, "Do I really need a partner to be successful?"

A typical mistake business partners make is bounding into business before getting to know each other. You need to be able to express your opinions, expectations, and ideas so you'll need to connect with your partner. Test the partnership by engaging in a minor project together. You can learn so much about personalities and core values when the project requires cooperation.

Be prudent when partnering with family members or close friends. Contemplate whether you're willing to risk damaging your relationship if the partnership collapses. Delicately prepare and plan for every facet in advance, so there's no question about how problematic situations will be managed. Clearly outline your expectations for how the business will operate and delegate roles and responsibilities of the partners based on their desires and competence.

Partnerships offer a greater amount of flexibility and can be an excellent way of linking different skills and to create a dominant business entity. Also, by bring in more people into the venture, it's easier to raise capital. Overall, business partnerships should be taking extremely seriously and with caution. Never dive into something without doing complete research on the other person's character.

30. TYPES OF PARTNERSHIPS

A "general partnership" is a company owned by two or more people who agree to run the company as co-owners. Each partner has an equal share of losses and profits, unless otherwise agreed. Partnership agreements play a considerable role in partnerships that don't evenly divide duties and shares. A partnership agreement is an important document that will need to be agreed upon by all partners. The agreement outlines the relationship between the partners, the ownership, and the duties of each partner. General partnerships are easy to enact, low-cost, and pliable. However, your personal assets are at risk and you're responsible for each other's actions.

"Limited partnerships" are more structured than "general" ones and have both limited and general partners. To start a limited partnership, you'll need at least one general and one limited partner. Limited partners serve as investors and usually do not have decision-making rights. They get ownership but won't have as many responsibilities and risks as a general partner. If you're a limited partner, be careful about the decisions you make and the things you do in the partnership.

If you would like to make it easy to add or remove partners and have liability protection from other members' actions, you should choose a "limited liability partnership". A limited liability partnership, or LLP, is a type of partnership where owners aren't held personally responsible for the debts of the business or other partners' actions. You generally can't lose your personal assets if someone takes legal action against your business, but partners can be held liable if they personally do something wrong. In some states, only certain professionals can form an LLP, so check your state's rules before you form a limited liability partnership.

Most businesses can form an LLC, or "limited liability company", and can have two or more owners, called members. With an LLC partnership, members' personal assets are protected and, in most cases, members can't be sued for the business' debts or actions. This type of partnership offers personal liability protection and tax flexibility for the members.

One of the first things you should do as a business owner is decide the type of business structure you want to set up. Be sure to measure the advantages and disadvantages before you decide the type of partnership that is best for your company. Lawyers and accountants will be helpful in this process.

31. BUSINESS TO BUSINESS (B2B) SALES

Business-to-Business marketing refers to companies who primarily sell services and products to businesses rather than directly to consumers. B2B marketing for small companies can be challenging. A narrow budget means marketing costs must be firmly controlled and returns must be validated by palpable data.

B2B sales may be more complex than B2C (business to consumers), but many of the same processes apply to B2B selling. To be a valuable salesman, you still need to generate leads, initiate contact, get their product or solution in front of the customer, and complete the sale. You need to know your market, competitors, and who their ideal customers are. You also need to know how your product or service fits into the marketplace and what your value proposition will be.

Part of a successful B2B sales process is finding your potential customers. These customers will be the decision makers with the authority and budget to buy your service or product. You should also assess and qualify your prospects to make sure they have the interest, need, and budget to buy. Now that you have researched your market, competition, and ideal customers, it's time to get in front of them. There are different way to do that in business-to-business sales, including social media, also known as outbound marketing. You could also do some inbound marketing by creating a company blog of interesting content that engages readers who turn into customers. Or try some direct marketing, which would entail mailing a brochure or cold-calling a prospect. If you utilize direct marketing for your B2B sales, follow-up emails should be part of your sales strategy. When doing a "follow-up", you should send over a business proposal or statement of work. Write the proposal soon after the pitch meeting so you can remember everything discussed and put it in writing.

Now it's time to close the sale. If you've made it this far in the process, this should be a painless step. The client wants to purchase your service or product, now you just need to get it in writing. If there is any reluctance to from the potential to client to close the sale, find out what concerns they still have, and figure out a solution. Perhaps it takes an addition product demo or meeting.

Put in the effort to build and sustain great relationships that lead to pleased clients who want to come back and purchase repeatedly. The goal of a successful B2B sales approach is to get more customers, including more longstanding ones. That's why it's vital to value relationships over sales, offer lasting solutions to suit your clients' needs, and take advantage of the right technology to support your sales efforts. You will start building relationships with your buyers and will gain their trust, and that's the key to succeeding in business-to-business sales.

32. CREATING VALUE

You create value for your customers by offering outstanding and fast service, offering your know-how at no cost, or giving customers an experience to remember. This is highly potent at expanding business and keeping it. Running a business is not about you, it's about your customers. The more you try to recognize the needs of your customers, you'll be able to provide a solution. In doing this, not only do you get a sale, but you get a long-term relationship going. Building rapport and trust with the customers is an extremely important part of running a company.

Free samples, add-ons, and convenience are classic examples of ways to create value for your customers. If the gift is something the customer didn't expect, this contributes to the delight factor. This creates a bond with the customer.

Providing useful content is also always a magnet for potential customers. You're offering them value and education. Equally, it establishes you as a source of authority in the industry you operate. Remember, your customers always come first. Without a loyal customer base, your business may not survive.

33. LOYTALTY PROGRAMS

Small business loyalty programs are designed to set up repeat business and harvest a flourishing network of brand ambassadors who sing your praises to their friends, family, and extended circles. A loyalty program rewards customers for their repeat business, but it can also include benefits for referrals, social sharing, and other actions that exhibit loyalty.

However, there are some costs linked with loyalty programs, including energy and time it takes to set one up as well as the rewards themselves. With some clever math and earnestness, you can get a program up and running with minimal costs and a high return on investment (ROI). What kind of loyalty programs are there? There are a few ways to think about this. How will customers actually access your program? Will they enter their information into a digital database or will they carry a rewards card that they present every time they shop with you?

Punch cards were the standard for a long time. You would give a card to customers and punch it, or stamp, every time they made a purchase. They can be a bit outdated these days, not to mention they're easy to lose and a hassle for the customer. Scannable membership cards are a step up from punch cards as there is two-way visibility into the customers's habits, but it's a physical item they need to carry with them. If you don't like those choices, you could try email marketing. This is a way to include your customers in a rewards program without them having to carry a card with them. Get their email in order to form a profile so you can keep track of their purchase history as well as send them additional updates about opportunities, like new items or sales. If you'd like to be more "modern", you could create a mobile app. A customized mobile app allows you to collect and organize customer data, so both sides have access to the customer's history and reward status. Most small companies will want a points-based program but more and more are gravitating towards email or mobile app formats. These combine with their existing customer service solutions and require minimal effort from the customer.

Whether you're looking to personalize your marketing efforts, boost retention, or build a bond with your customers, a loyalty program is an all-in-one solution that is generally worth the investment. Great loyalty programs help you construct a bond with your customers by giving them rewards that go beyond a "discount on your next purchase". Start

your search for a program that suits your budget and
needs today.

34. INVESTMENTS

Small entrepreneurs are used to taking risks, but
when it comes to investing, taking risks can put your
business in a perilous position. Your company is your
most sizeable asset and main source of income, so
you don't need to take any unnecessary risks.
Investments is one of the safest ways to increase your
money quickly.

One of the most crucial investment strategies for
small business owners is investing back into your
business. Nonetheless, you need to establish limits
since fixating your capital in one asset can be awfully
risky. If something happens to your company, your
personal finances could be in danger. You need to
find a satisfying balance between reinvesting in your
own business and investing in outside opportunities.

Make sure not to be single-minded when choosing
where you're investing. Regularly, small business
owners grow a bias towards their own industry due to
comfort and familiarity, and only invest in their area

of expertise. You need to diversify your investment portfolio. This will reduce the overall risk since some investment may be up while other are on a downturn. Build a limited investment in your own industry. If problems arise in your industry, your business and the rest of your portfolio could suffer gravely. You should put your investments in an assortment of sectors and industries. Even if you only have a small amount of capital to invest with, it's important to start investing.

Don't follow the unusually common philosophy of risking a large sum of money. Allocating small amounts of what you're saving and diversifying your investments provides a much lower risk than risking a large sum in one investment. By investing small amounts routinely, your portfolio can grow rampantly.

Don't neglect investing into your retirement. When you own your own business, you have no employer to provide a 401(k) so you'll need to open and contribute to a retirement plan. There are different types of tax-deferred retirement options to help you set aside money. Start saving as soon as possible and try your best to contribute the maximum allowable amount each year.

Learning to invest can lead to better profits and a better understanding of the importance of diversifying your investments. There are related risks with investing, but there are plenty of safe options that can eliminate potential risk down the line. The risk is worth taking once you're able to see the swell in potential for the returns on your investments.

35. TIME MANAGEMENT

Time is your greatest commodity, that's why you need to use it wisely. Before doing anything, you should complete at least one day of time logging. Track everything you do from the moment you wake up until you go to bed. Behave normally on this day and treat it like a typical workday for you.

From there, you can easily see where time is being wasted and you can determine the percentage of time you spend on each activity. The intention is to find where your spending way too much time. Categories to consider are: phone calls, meetings, email, breaks, errands, and other nonproductive tasks.

A very affective way to calculate where you should spend more time is the 80/20 rule. This rule says that 80% of your results come from 20% of your efforts. Effective time management increases the amount of time each day and each week in that 20% category where you're going to get the best results in your business.

36. HAVE A ROUTINE

The core production of doing things for your company will take up the majority of your day. However, it's critical to make time for other valuable things, like building skills, networking, and recreation. Your time is a precious asset.

Start your day early and get in a healthy breakfast and maybe a quick workout. Getting your blood pumping will give your mood and productivity a boost. After you've worked out, eaten, and showered now you can focus on your core production time. This is when you should focus on the priorities that need to get done first for your business to stay afloat.

After a long day, it's important to unwind and take some time to relax. You can't put your best foot forward if you're mentally and physically drained. Find a positive routine that fits your lifestyle and incorporate it into your daily life. Keeping a routine will help keep you on track for success.

37. WORKING LONG HOURS

Having your own business has many upsides and powerful motivators, but the reality is a little less glamorous. Be prepared to work 50+ hours a week, especially when first starting up. Despite the long hours, most business owners don't complain. To them, it's well worth the struggle so they can live their dreams.

Long hours tend to spill into other parts of your life, like vacations. Even when small business owners are on vacation, most of them will check in to work at least once a day. It's not all bad news, though. Vacations tend to be longer if you've been in business for a while and have more employees.

Many entrepreneurs find themselves working odd hours of the day. They don't follow a standard 9-5, 40-hour workweek. Many aspiring business owners often want to know how many hours they should be working each week. The truth is, there are no set number of hours you need to work. Hours worked don't necessarily equate to success. Some owners can find success working 30 hours or fewer, while other owners may have to work 50 hours to reach that same achievement.

38. BUILD A SUPPORT NETWORK

Being an entrepreneur can get a bit lonely. With the hardship of risks and decisions falling on your lap, you need a capable support network that can offer understanding and advice.Building a network takes energy and effort, but you'll need to commit the time. When you're first starting out, you may want to meet potential mentors. Look for accomplished leaders and ask them to join you for drinks or coffee.

You can try hosting or joining social events which would help you meet other like-minded individuals, as well. Invite people in your network to a cocktail or dinner party and ask each person to bring someone you've never met. You'll get to know your peers much better and have a chance to make new connections.

As your support network builds, ask yourself "what to I have to offer?". You must give to get so be charitable when others need advice or introductions. Offer them your support, pay for drinks after work and applaud their small wins. Your support will add up and make them much more generous with theirs.

Remember to make time for old friends, too. Those are the ones most likely to give you unconditional support, whether or not they have any experience in your industry. However, you need to show that you value the relationship even when you're busy with work. If you want your friends to be there when you need them, you should devote some time every week to grab a drink, watch a baseball game, or to just say hi. You need not commit a lot of time if you're overburdened, but it is important to give them some work-free time.

39. INVEST IN YOURSELF

Overlooking the fact that you need to invest in yourself, as well as your business, is very common. You are the fuel that keeps the business headed in the right direction. Taking online courses is one of the easiest ways to invest in yourself. They allow you to continue learning new skills that will make your life easier as a business owner. Obtaining a certificate will expand your service offering and hike revenue.

Listen to podcasts that entertain and educate you during downtime. You can listen to podcasts to get advice from other entrepreneurs or learn about certain subjects. The great thing about podcasts is you can listen to them anywhere. Driving in your car, taking a bath, cooking dinner are all great times to turn on something to expand your knowledge. If podcasts aren't your "thing", there are boundless amounts of reading material. Absorb motivational material to keep you driven and inspired or read educational books to grow your skills.

Investing in yourself also means taking care of yourself mentally and physically. You can't do your best work if you're neglecting yourself. Make sure to get plenty of exercise and eat a well-balanced diet. Exercise will boost endorphins, stabilize your mood, and help with focus. At the end of a long day, take a relaxing bath or shower and wash away the stress of the day.

40. GET ENOUGH SLEEP

Not getting adequate sleep shrinks your mental abilities and clouds thought processes and decision-making. Lack of sleep makes you irritable and causes you to do things you may not do if you were thinking with a clearer head. As a business owner, your employees, suppliers, partners, and customers rely on you to make the best decisions. Purposely not taking care of yourself is violating the responsibility you assume when you choose to lead.

There are people who suffer from insomnia and that can be challenging to treat, but there are others who often stay up too late to watch a movie or game, do more work, or have another drink. This can push your body too far. Try to make it a point to have the lights, televisions, and phones turned off at a decent hour. Have that last cup of coffee at lunch instead of dinner and stop having that last glass of wine late in the night. Sure, you may not fall asleep right away, but relaxing and deep breathing in a dark, quiet room can be meditative.

As a business owner, you are required to be mentally and physically alert. The smartest business owners are balanced and understand the benefits of moderation. Go to bed; the world will continue to turn and you'll be more competent to deal with tomorrow's challenges.

41. MANAGE YOUR EMOTIONS

You will need to learn to control your emotions so your emotions don't control you. Everyone is human and emotions naturally come up in day-to-day life. You may not be able to control what you feel, but you are capable of controlling what you do with these emotions. You can make much more perceptive and well thought-out decisions when you're not ruled by emotions.

Your emotions influence your perception, even if you don't realize it. Once you've figured this out, you'll have the ability to reframe your awareness and change your attitude. By removing emotions from the equation, you'll gain better insight, which will help you focus on the big picture.

Staying calm amidst adversity can be difficult, especially when fear and anger arise. The more you practice separating yourself from emotions, the more calm and collected you'll be. When something goes

wrong, take a step back and observe what you're
feeling.

42. BUILDING YOUR CONFIDENCE

In business, there will always be times when
you're forced to step out of your comfort zone and
you may feel less than confident when first starting
out in the business world. One method to develop
your confidence is to enact objectives. Having a
concise vision of what you want your business to
become, you will be in a developed position to work
toward that goal. As you establish measurable
objectives, it is possible to view your progress and
that will facilitate more confidence.

Negativity has the ability to lower confidence and
reduce motivation. When you surround yourself with
good energy and positive people, you will
automatically be more productive. Have a group of
positive influences you can count on for support when
you're feeling shaky and off track.

Revel in the small accomplishments. Give yourself
a pat on the back when you make that initial sale.
When you graciously and fearlessly tackle a

demanding situation, celebrate. Little victorious moments will serve as a reminder of just how talented and worthy you are. No one is born confident. Confidence has to be learned and cultivated. Others may help on your path to self-confidence, but it's ultimately up to you.

43. HAVING MOTIVATION

Identifying your motivation before starting a business is very important. When challenges arise and test your determination, it's difficult to stay focused if you don't know why you're doing something. Understanding and knowing what motivates you can help you avoid getting overwhelmed and generate the feeling you are prepared for anything.

You need to find transparency in why you're doing what you're doing, what the risks are, and what you hope to accomplish. If you haven't taken the time to think it through, it can be a struggle to figure out your motivation. There are a slew of different motivations including money, pride, passion, credibility, family, and society.

Once you realize your motivation, you'll be ready to push through and make difficult decisions. You'll have clarity and a foundation and you'll be less likely to lose focus. When you understand what motivates you, you will have the confidence you need when starting your company.

44. LEARN FROM FAILURES

Most people view success as positive and failure as negative. However, failure is not a bad thing. You can grow, evolve, and learn from past blunders. You will learn valuable life lessons as you go through life and encounter failures.

The breathtaking feeling of loss and failure is curbed by staying humble. Being humble makes you mentally prepared for failure when it comes your way. Don't be afraid to be liable when you're responsible for a business failure.

Don't be afraid of change. Sometimes you have to make drastic changes when you fail. When things aren't going the way you had hoped and planned, you have to sit back and look at the changes that need to be made and embrace them. There can't be success without failure. You're going to fail at one point or another, it's inevitable. Take the time to reorganize your thoughts after a collapse and realize what you did wrong. How people handle failure determines how successful they will be.

45. DEALING WITH CYNICS

Not everyone will be in your corner. You'll find pessimists who are continually offering opinions on what you should do, or more regularly, not do. You'll meet naysayers along the way, but there are ways to negate their negativity.

Pessimists generally have opinions about everything. Dig a little deeper and you'll very likely discover that they've rarely attempted anything in their own personal lives. So, if you're hearing from someone who has nothing but negative things to say, consider the source.

That being said, critics are never entirely wrong, so when you hear criticism, ask what part of it may be legitimate. You should have the humility to learn from anyone, even critics. However, as much as you may want to learn from those cynical people, you're likely wasting your breath in trying to change their mind. Most of the time, it's best to just thank them for their outlook and move on. Moving on and building a better future for yourself is the best way to win a battle with a cynic. Results have a way of speaking for themselves and usually silence the critics.

46. WEARING MULTIPLE HATS

Like most business owners, your business card might carry the title of CEO, but you know on any given day it could just as easily read marketing manager, accountant, sales associate, or customer support representative. The success of your business leans on your ability to wear the multiple hats needed to keep the wheels of your company turning. Whether you see this as a curse or a blessing, you need to set a plan for success.

The first step is distinguishing all the diverse aspects of your business that you're currently managing. Identify your separate responsibilities, which include operational tasks and income-generating ones. Effective goal setting is key to success, and you should set individual goals for each facet of your company.

Getting lost in the daily grind of your business (working "in" your business) and putting off long-term, strategic planning (working "on" your business) can be all too easy for a small entrepreneur. If you find yourself in this position, you'll need to dedicate time each week to consider your business and market trends, think about potential opportunities, and do some long-term positioning. Make sure you're making time to work "on" your business and not just work "in" your business.

When you're used to running your business on your own, it can be challenging to relinquish control of day-to-day details, but it's crucial to let go. Successful leaders don't micromanage what everyone else is doing. Instead, they empower people around them to do their jobs. Give your employees and contractors the freedom to make decisions, even letting them make mistakes and correcting those mistakes themselves. In the long run, you'll have a more confident, more effective, and more capable workforce.

47. DEALING WITH LAZY EMPLOYEES

The business you run is only as good as the employees you hire. If you're lucky, you find good, responsible employees. You're not so lucky if you've dealt with toxic ones. What about those employees that aren't toxic but still underperform?

Usually, with a lazy employee, the best thing to do is address it head-on. You may be a little hesitant to speak with him, or her, and you're likely aware that the employee may get defensive, but it is your job to do your best to dodge a showdown. No one wants to admit they've been lazy, especially when a paycheck is on the line.

Use time sheets as a record of time in and out if the problem is with consistent tardiness. Document complaints from coworkers but when referencing them to the employee make it vague enough so they won't know who complained about them. Having specific incidences cataloged ahead of time will help avoid arguing about the details about their work behavior. The lack of motivation could stem from a feeling that their contribution to the business is too small. If this happens to be the case, there are paths you can take to motivate your team member. Offer more training, opportunities for advancement, delegate more responsibilities and notice when they excel. This will make the employee feel like he has something to contribute and will motivate him to be a better team member.

48. CUSTOMER SERVICE EXCELLENCE

For any sized business, customer service is one of the most efficient ways to build and preserve a competitive advantage. With small businesses, there is more at stake. When you're small, disappointed customers are, potentially, a catastrophe, and every charmed customer has the ability to provide your business with the most important marketing you could receive.

Running a business is not about you, it's about your customers. You need to put the customers at the center of everything, including how you schedule your time, how you design and refine your processes, and how you nurture the ones you already have. Customer service is about being present, from the service counter to emails. Don't take hours or days to respond to your customers. This will no doubt leave them feeling neglected and unhappy with your services.

If you're a small business owner, you have the opportunity to personalize the customer experience. Get to know them by name, remember faces, and regularly reach out to your customers. By doing this, you are making interactions with your business more impressive and will make your customers feel appreciated. However, don't make false promises. Flashy promotions and pledges will definitely attract customers, but nothing is more disheartening for potential and current customers than click-bait offers or promotions with multiple stipulations. Be upfront and honest about your promises, and you'll produce a happier customer base. Overall, delivering superb customer service will help you keep your customers happy, boost your small business, and handle mistakes without losing a customer's business.

49. CONS OF RUNNING A BUSINESS

Running a business can bring about a new kind of stress. Unlike an employee, you are responsible for all decisions. You can fail or succeed and everyone will be looking at you. Just as you can be looked at as a leader, you can also be seen as irresponsible, so it's imperative to make good decisions. Stress can also be intense if you do not make a dependable income.

It's difficult to draw a line between "work" and "life" when you are your own boss and work-life balance can become tricky. Having to wear many hats all at once may force you to do sales calls in the evening, finish important paperwork on the weekend, or answering business emails before bed. Taking care of all responsibilities as an entrepreneur while maintaining a balanced life can be difficult, but it is probably worth it.

Risk is a big disadvantage of running a company. Failure, debt, risk of bankruptcy, and hungry competitors all are factors to consider. The first few years of the business may not offer much disposable income and this can affect your individual banking and lead to trouble with car payments, mortgages, and other essentials. Some business owners start out in debt because they had to borrow money in order to cover start-up costs.

50. PROS OF BEING AN ENTREPRENEUR

There are so many motivators for becoming a business owner. Being an entrepreneur means you can take control of your own destiny. You're not relying on your boss' decisions for how the company performs, or that the boss will choose to keep you employed. All the decisions, no matter how small or big, are now under your management. Where and how you work and how much money you make is fully your choice. Controlling your own destiny is liberating and empowering.

When you get to do what you love, it doesn't really feel like the work you used to know. Although you may not enjoy every task of the journey, you get to choose to work on something you care about. You get to live your purpose and because you're passionate about your work, you'll really do your best.

You can establish a great legacy and leave your mark on the world. You get to motivate and lead others by your example. You're already aware that you are competent of more and aren't being compensated enough. Starting your own business is about maximizing your contribution. You really get to magnify the impact you have when you free yourself from working for someone else. You'll never want to do anything else once you have a taste for entrepreneurship.

"EntreLeadership", Dave Ramsey

"The Lean Startup", Eric Ries

"Crushing It!", Gary Vaynerchuck

READ OTHER

50 THINGS TO KNOW

BOOKS

50 Things to Know to Get Things Done Fast: Easy Tips for Success

50 Things to Know About Going Green: Simple Changes to Start Today

50 Things to Know to Live a Happy Life Series

50 Things to Know to Organize Your Life: A Quick Start Guide to Declutter, Organize, and Live Simply

50 Things to Know About Being a Minimalist: Downsize, Organize, and Live Your Life

50 Things to Know About Speed Cleaning: How to Tidy Your Home in Minutes

50 Things to Know About Choosing the Right Path in Life

50 Things to Know to Get Rid of Clutter in Your Life: Evaluate, Purge, and Enjoy Living

50 Things to Know About Journal Writing: Exploring Your Innermost Thoughts & Feelings

50 Things to Know

Stay up to date with new releases on Amazon:
https://amzn.to/2VPNGr7

Mailing List: Join the 50 Things to Know
Mailing List to Learn About New Releases

50 Things to Know

Please leave your honest review of this book on Amazon and Goodreads. We appreciate your positive and constructive feedback. Thank you.